Step-by-Step
Decorative Painting

Judy Balchin

Search Press

First published in Great Britain 2001

Search Press Limited
Wellwood, North Farm Road,
Tunbridge Wells, Kent TN2 3DR

Reprinted 2002, 2004, 2005

ISBN 0 85532 910 6

Suppliers

If you have difficulty in obtaining any of the materials and equipment mentioned in this book, then please visit the Search Press website for details of suppliers: www.searchpress.com

Alternatively, you can write to the Publishers at the address above, for a current list of stockists, which includes firms who operate a mail-order service.

Acknowledgements

The Publishers would like to thank the Bridgeman Art Library for permission to reproduce the photograph on page 5.

Printed in China by WKT Company Ltd

To my daughters Rebecca and Ruth for being there

A big thank you to John Wright of Pebeo UK Ltd., Unit 109, Solent Business Centre, Millbrook Road West, Millbrook, Southampton, SO15 0HW for supplying the paints used in this book.

My thanks also to the team at Search Press whose constant encouragement and sense of humour made the writing of this book a pleasure – in particular, Editorial Director Roz Dace, Editor Chantal Roser, Designer Tamsin Hayes and Photographer Lotti de la Bédoyère.

The Publishers would like to say a huge thank you to Letitia Thomas, Karina Luke, Lorna Perry, Nicole Fields, Guy Pitchers, Luke Hunter and Martin Baker.

Special thanks are also due to Southborough Primary School, Tunbridge Wells.

When this sign is used in the book, it means that adult supervision is needed.

REMEMBER!
Ask an adult to help you when you see this sign.

Contents

Introduction

So what exactly is meant by decorative painting? Well, let us try to imagine a world where it does not exist – where all surfaces are plain with no decoration. Difficult, isn't it? For thousands of years, people have had an irresistible desire to decorate things, from cave walls and pottery to buildings, furniture and fabrics. Throughout history we have been attracted to pattern and colour, and today you only have to look around your own home, or visit your local shopping centre, to see a wonderful variety of decorative colours and shapes.

Before starting the projects in this book, take a little time to look at the types of decoration used by different civilisations and countries. Each one has its own colour preferences and style. This can be seen when you look at floral designs. Flowers have always been popular as a subject, but compare the simple, stylish Lotus flower designs of ancient Egyptian artists with the intricate blossoms created by the Chinese. Both are beautiful, but very different.

You do not have to look far to find things to decorate and you do not have to spend a lot of money on them. We use flowers to decorate a box in the following pages, but we also have great fun decorating eggs with monsters and pebbles with animals. Wooden spoons are decorated with insects and colourful patchwork squares are painted on a glass jar to transform it into a fancy sweet container.

I will show you how to paint on different surfaces, including wood, paper, cardboard, terracotta, glass and stone. All the objects can be found easily, in or around your home. Cardboard boxes, paper plates, used containers and many other objects can be transformed with a little paint and some imagination. Acrylic paints have been used in every project, as these are inexpensive, cover the surface and are hard-wearing.

I have had great fun writing this book, and hope that as you work through the projects you will think of other ways of decorating surfaces. Look out for unusual things to paint. Be bold with your designs, use bright colours and have lots of fun!

***Opposite** Chinese craft workers are famous for their decorated porcelain, which is a form of white pottery. This dog was made in the 17th century: the unpainted dog would have been fired to make it hard before the colourful decoration was applied.*

Materials

The best thing about decorative painting is that it does not cost much to get started. You only need some of the things shown on this page to begin. You may already have some acrylic paints and brushes. You can find many of the other things in your own home. You do need an egg cup, plastic eyes, fabric and ribbons for some of the projects. Check the list of things you need carefully at the start of each project.

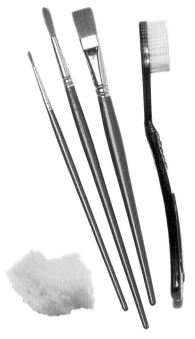

You can paint on all sorts of things and all kinds of surfaces with acrylic paints. Paper, card and cardboard are ideal, but so are **terracotta** and glass. You can also paint on eggshell, pebbles and wood.

Use different size paintbrushes to apply paint. You can also use sponge to apply paint. Use a toothbrush to spray paint.

Acrylic paints are hard-wearing and easy to use. It is best to use these paints from a palette. Use varnish to give a shiny appearance.

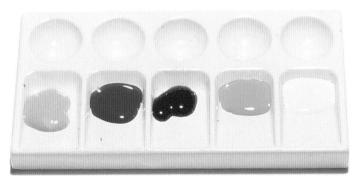

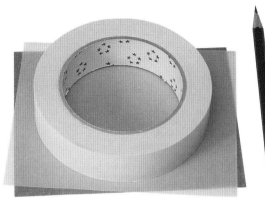

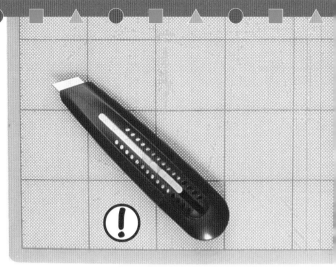

Tracing paper, transfer paper and a pencil are used to transfer designs. Masking tape should be used to hold the designs in place. This can also mask areas when painting and secure loops of string to the back of projects.

A craft knife is used to cut plastic or thick card. Always ask an adult to do this for you as they are very sharp. Craft knives should be used on a cutting mat.

PVA glue is used to glue objects on to surfaces, or to stick surfaces together.

Scissors are used to cut paper, card and string.

String is ideal for making hanging loops which are secured to the back of projects.

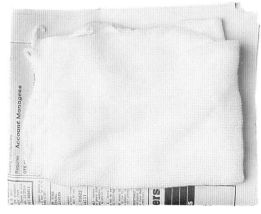

Sheets of newspaper can be used to cover your work surface. An old cloth provides a stable base for a curved object that requires painting.

Thin card (for example, from a cereal packet) or thick card are ideal as a base for a project. Mirror card can be used if you want to make a fun mirror (see page 26).

Techniques

Decorative painting is not difficult to do, but it is worth reading through this section carefully before you start. The techniques are demonstrated on a cardboard box. Always clean brushes thoroughly in water after using them.

Note Decorative painting can be messy so it is best to cover your work surface with a large piece of newspaper.

Painting

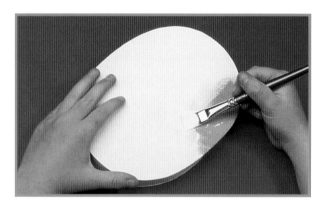

Use a flat brush to paint large surfaces. This gives an even finish which is easier to work on. Sometimes, you may need to apply two coats of paint, so the surface is well covered. Allow the first coat to dry before applying the second.

Splattering

Protect the work surface with newspaper. Dilute some paint on a palette with water so that it is runny. Dip the bristles of a toothbrush in the paint. Hold the toothbrush with the bristles towards the surface you are decorating and run your finger along the brush. This will splatter random paint spots on to the surface.

Masking and sponging

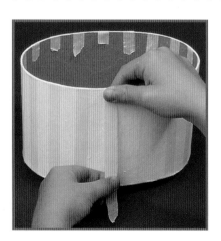

To mask areas of an object, press strips of masking tape on to the surface. Make sure that the edges of the tape are smoothed flat. The masked areas will remain the base colour.

When sponging, pour a little paint on to a palette. Dip the sponge in the paint, then dab the surfaces of the base and lid all over. Remove the masking tape to reveal neat stripes.

Stencilling, painting and outlining

Now that the surfaces have been prepared with flat colour and textured effects, images can be added. Stencils are a quick and easy way to create pictures which can then be added to and outlined.

1 Tape the stencil to the surface with small pieces of masking tape. Use a sponge to dab the paint through the stencil. Remove the stencil.

2 Paint in the pattern using a small paintbrush. Pull the brush towards you smoothly, lifting it off the surface as you complete the stroke to create a neat shape.

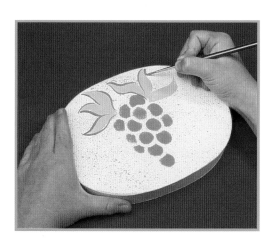

3 Outlining with black paint makes images really stand out. For this design, use a small round paintbrush to outline the leaves and the left-hand side of the grapes. This will create a three-dimensional effect.

Bumble Bee Spoon

The insect world is fascinating and amazing. Think of the bee, the ladybird and the butterfly – they are all so different. Their amazing range of shapes and colours is not accidental. The insects use them as a defence against enemies and to attract other insects. In this project a bee motif is used to decorate a wooden spoon, and the same colours are used on the handle. Wood is a wonderfully smooth surface to paint on. If your spoon is a little rough, sand it down with sandpaper before starting.

YOU WILL NEED

Wooden spoon
Coloured acrylic paint
Large and small paintbrushes
Varnish • Tracing paper
Transfer paper
Masking tape • Pencil
Coloured ribbon

1 Transfer the pattern on page 29 on to the back of the spoon (see page 28).

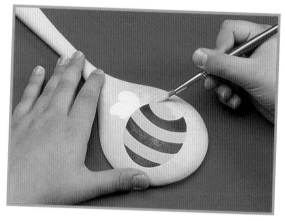

2 Paint the black stripes and then paint the bee's body and head using a small paintbrush and a light colour. Leave to dry.

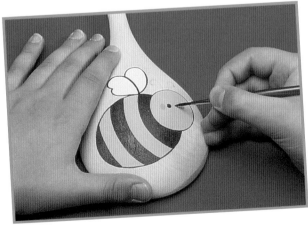

3

Paint the bee's cheeks, then carefully outline the bee in a dark colour. Paint in the eyes, mouth and antennae.

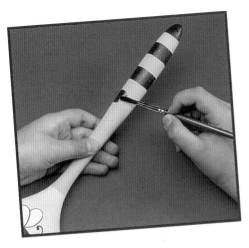

4

Paint the handle in the lighter colour. When it is dry, paint in the darker stripes.

5

Use a larger paintbrush to varnish the back of the spoon. When the varnish is dry, turn the spoon over and repeat on the front.

6 Tie a coloured ribbon around the handle so that you can hang it up.

Note This bumble bee spoon is purely decorative and should not be used to cook or eat with.

FURTHER IDEAS
Copy paintings of other brightly coloured insects and make your own colony of insect spoons.

Kosy Gift Box

Artists have painted and decorated surfaces with flowers for a long time, inspired by the beautiful colours and shapes they have found in nature. Many fine examples of flower paintings can be found in museums and art galleries. These simple roses are easy to paint. They are used to transform a plain cardboard container into a lovely gift box. Look for an old box to decorate – you do not have to buy one.

 Use a large brush to paint the box and lid with a pale colour. You may need to apply two coats if the first one does not cover the surface completely. Make sure that the first coat is dry before applying the second.

 Pour a small amount of a darker colour into a palette. Dip the sponge in the paint and dab it around the base and rim of the lid. Leave to dry.

Using a smaller brush and the same colour, paint circles all over the lid and box. Leave to dry.

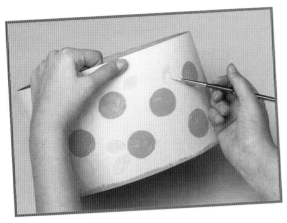

 Paint leaf shapes around the circles using a different colour. Try to fill in any gaps. Leave to dry.

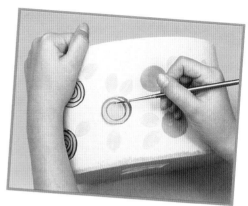

 Decorate each coloured circle with a large swirl using black paint and a small paintbrush. Allow to dry.

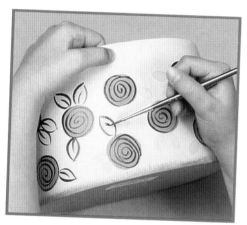

 Outline the leaves with black paint and add a vein line down the centre of each one.

FURTHER IDEAS

Decorate boxes with different flowers – daisies, sunflowers and poppies. Keep the designs simple and use bright colours.

Sun Wall Hanging

Astrology is the study of the Sun, Moon, planets and stars, and the way they influence our lives. Astrological symbols have been used as decoration by artists and craftspeople throughout the ages. The Sun is ninety-three million miles away from Earth, but you can bring it right into your own home by creating this colourful Sun wall hanging. A paper plate is the perfect round blank on which to work. The basic design is painted and then decorated with dots and swirls of metallic paint.

YOU WILL NEED

Paper plate
Coloured and metallic acrylic paint
Large and small paintbrushes
Tracing paper • Transfer paper
Masking tape • Pencil
Scissors • String

Note Place your plate over a roll of masking tape. This will help support the plate when you are painting it.

1 Using a large paintbrush, paint the centre of the plate in a light colour and the border in a dark colour. Leave to dry.

2 Transfer the pattern on page 29 on to the centre of the plate (see page 28). Using a small paintbrush, outline the features in a dark colour, then paint in the eyes and cheeks. Leave to dry.

3 Paint the eyebrows, eyelids, lips and chin with a lighter colour. Allow to dry.

 Use a pencil to draw the Sun's rays around the border. Carefully cut them out.

Decorate the Sun's face with dotted swirls of metallic paint. Add dotted swirls to the rays. Leave to dry.

 Tape a loop of string to the back of the top ray so that you can hang up your Sun.

FURTHER IDEAS

Make Moon and star wall hangings to complement your Sun — or decorate lots of small plates and create a matching mobile.

Patchwork Sweet Jar

For generations, people have created patchwork using scraps and odd remnants of material. You may have seen beautifully stitched quilts made in this way. They are usually made to commemorate an event or special occasion, such as a wedding. In this project we use paint to create our own patchwork. An old glass jar is decorated and transformed into a stylish sweet container. Look for a large jar to show off your painting. Do not forget to wash and dry it thoroughly before you begin.

YOU WILL NEED
Large glass jar
Black and white acrylic paint
Coloured acrylic paint
Large and small paintbrushes
Pencil • Varnish • Sweets
Coloured fabric • Scissors
Elastic band
Coloured ribbon

 Paint the jar with two coats of white paint using a large brush. Leave an unpainted square in the middle, so when the jar is finished you can see what is in it. Let the first coat of paint dry before applying the second coat.

 Use a pencil to divide the jar up into squares.

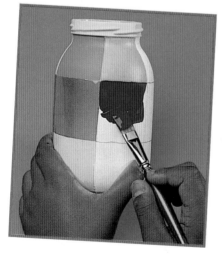

 Paint the neck of the jar using a large paintbrush and a bright colour. When the jar is dry, paint in the squares using different colours. Leave to dry.

5 Add stitch lines around each square using a fine paintbrush and black paint. Leave to dry, then paint a coat of varnish on to the jar using a large brush.

4 Decorate each square with dots, lines or hearts. Try to make each one different.

FURTHER IDEAS
Recycle old bottles and create colourful patchwork patterns on them — or decorate other glass objects.

6 Fill the jar with sweets. Cut out a circle of fabric double the size of the top of the jar. Secure the fabric around the top with an elastic band. Finally, tie a ribbon over the elastic band.

Padlocked Money Box

This project uses *trompe l'oeil*, a French term that means 'deception of the eye'. It refers to something that looks real, but is not – it is just an illusion. The padlock and chain on this money box look real, but they are just painted on. Painted shadow lines and highlights make them look three-dimensional.

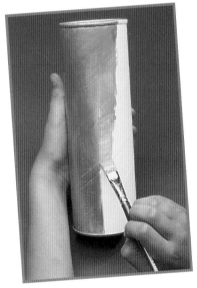

 Paint the tube with white paint using a large brush and allow it to dry. You may have to apply a few coats of paint to cover any lettering. Wait for the last coat to dry, then apply two coats of metallic paint.

2 Cover the work surface with sheets of newspaper. Lay the tube on top. Pour small amounts of black and white paint into a palette and dilute them both with water. Using a toothbrush, splatter the tube first with white, then with black paint (see page 8). Roll the tube to make sure that you splatter the whole surface.

3 Transfer the pattern on page 30 on to the tube and fill it in with metallic paint. Leave to dry.

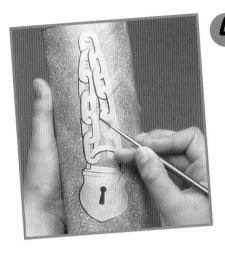

4 Using a small paintbrush, paint the keyhole. Add black shadow lines down the left-hand side and along the bottom of the chain links and padlock. Leave to dry.

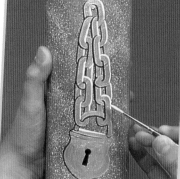

5

Paint white lines down the right-hand side and along the tops of the links and padlock, to create highlights.

6 Cut a slot in the top of the lid with a craft knife, then place the lid on top of the tube.

A craft knife is very sharp; it should always be used with a cutting mat. Ask an adult to help you.

FURTHER IDEAS

Design some symbols that mean 'Keep out', 'Private', 'Danger' and use these to decorate your money box.

Tiger Paperweight

Decorating pebbles or stones is an unusual and fascinating craft, and it is easy to do. Part of the fun is finding just the right shape. Look for a pebble or stone that suggests the shape of a tiger, and make sure that it has a smooth surface, as this will be easier to paint. Keep your design simple and use bold colours for the best effect.

YOU WILL NEED
Pebble
White and black acrylic paint
Coloured acrylic paint
Large and small paintbrushes
Pencil • 2 plastic eyes
PVA glue

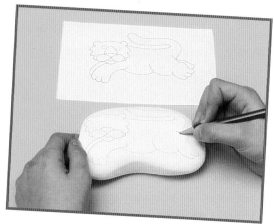

1 Paint the pebble white using a large paintbrush. Leave to dry. Copy the pattern from page 30 on to the pebble using a pencil.

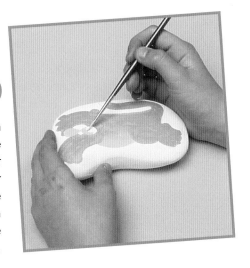

2 Using an appropriate colour, paint in the darker areas of the body, then paint in the lighter areas.

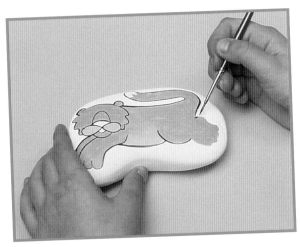

3 Outline the tiger using a small paintbrush and black paint.

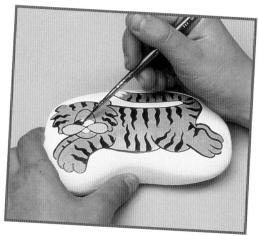

4 Add the stripes, nose and mouth using a small paintbrush and black paint. Leave to dry.

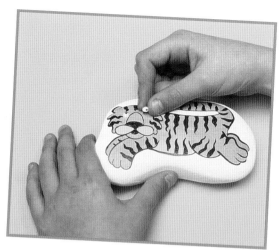

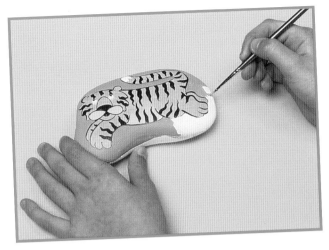

5 Glue on the plastic eyes using PVA glue. Leave to dry.

6 Paint the rest of the pebble in a bright colour. Leave to dry.

FURTHER IDEAS
Look for pebbles with unusual shapes and create your own animals and birds.

Fruity Flower Pot

Artists and craft workers have always used fruit motifs as decoration because of the amazing variety of shapes and colours they offer. Try making a list of all the fruits you can think of, and you will soon realise what a wonderful choice there is – oranges, apples, strawberries, lemons, grapes and more! This fruity project combines masking with sponging and stencilling – easy techniques that transform a plain terracotta pot into a colourful decorative plant container. Use an inexpensive sponge and tear pieces off as you need them.

YOU WILL NEED

Terracotta pot
Coloured acrylic paint
Large paintbrush • Palette
Thin card • Tracing paper
Transfer paper
Narrow masking tape
Pencil • Sponge • Scissors
Old cloth

 Paint the pot in a light colour using a large paintbrush. Leave to dry. Apply vertical strips of masking tape around the pot (see page 8). Try to make the gaps between the strips the same.

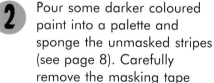 Pour some darker coloured paint into a palette and sponge the unmasked stripes (see page 8). Carefully remove the masking tape and leave to dry.

 Carefully sponge the top of the rim and the base of the pot with a different colour.

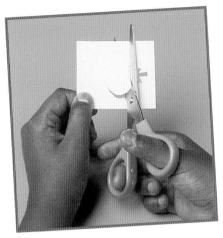

5

Lay the pot down on an old cloth to stop it rolling around. Tape the stencil on to the pot with masking tape.

4 Transfer the strawberry pattern on page 29 on to thin card. Cut out the strawberry shape to create a stencil.

6 Sponge paint through the stencil on to the pot. Choose two appropriate colours and use two pieces of sponge to colour the top of the strawberry, then the fruit. Work around the pot varying the angle of the strawberries.

FURTHER IDEAS
Change your designs by painting horizontal stripes around your pot and choose other types of fruit.

Monster Egg

An artist called Carl Fabergé created beautifully decorated eggs in the late nineteenth century. Some of his more precious jewelled eggs were made for the Russian royal family. I have used a hard boiled egg for this project and created an optical illusion. Although the monster is painted on the surface of the egg, it looks as though he is living inside it! If you want projects to last a long time, polystyrene or papier mâché eggs can be decorated using the same techniques.

YOU WILL NEED

Hard boiled egg
Black acrylic paint
Coloured acrylic paint
Large and small paintbrushes
Pencil • Egg cup

!

Ask an adult to boil the egg for you before you start the project.

1 Paint the top half of the egg in a colour of your choice using a large paintbrush. Sit it in an egg cup and leave it to dry. Turn it over and paint the bottom half. Leave to dry. Take care not to get paint on the egg cup.

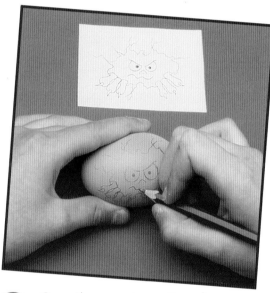

2 Copy the monster pattern from page 30 on to the egg using a pencil.

3

Paint the fingers using a brighter colour. Mix a touch of black with this colour to darken it and paint in the nose and eyes with a small paintbrush. The darker colour will make it look as though the monster is hiding in a shadowy hole.

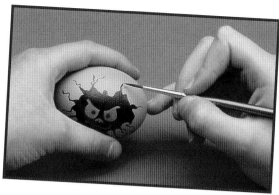

4 Add the claws, mouth and staring eyes using another bright colour.

5 Fill in the area behind the monster's features using black paint. Outline the fingers with the same paint, then add the lines around the edge of the hole.

Paint a thin white line along one side and along the bottom of the hole. Paint small white dots at the base of the fingers. This gives the appearance of highlights which makes the monster look even more three-dimensional.

6

FURTHER IDEAS

Use metallic acrylic paints to create realistic alien eggs, or invent your own monster.

Picasso Mirror

This project is inspired by the work of the Spanish artist, Pablo Picasso. He was born in 1881 and was one of the greatest painters of the twentieth century. You can use the style and colours of his work to create your own masterpiece. Before you start, take time to look at Picasso's work.

YOU WILL NEED

Thick card
Coloured acrylic paint
Black acrylic paint
Small paintbrush • Tracing paper
Transfer paper • Masking tape
Pencil • Craft knife • Scissors
Cutting mat • Mirror card
PVA glue • String

 Transfer the pattern from page 31 on to card (see page 28). Using bright colours and a small paintbrush, start filling in the design.

2 Continue painting the frame until all the areas are filled in.

 Outline the design using black paint. Leave to dry. Cut off the outer unpainted border using a craft knife. Cut out the unpainted central section.

 A craft knife is very sharp and it should always be used with a cutting mat. Make sure you ask an adult to help you when you use it.

 Paint the outside and inside edges of the cut card black.

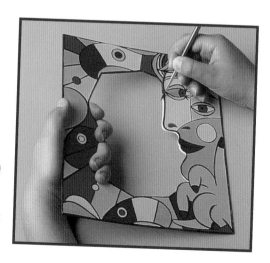

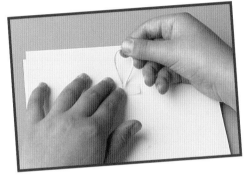

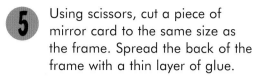

5 Using scissors, cut a piece of mirror card to the same size as the frame. Spread the back of the frame with a thin layer of glue.

6

Carefully press the frame down on to the mirror card, matching all the corners. Leave to dry.

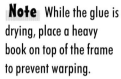

Note While the glue is drying, place a heavy book on top of the frame to prevent warping.

7 Tape a loop of string to the back of the frame with masking tape, so that you can hang up your mirror.

FURTHER IDEAS

Look at the work of other famous artists. Decorate photograph frames or mirror frames in their style.

Patterns

You can trace the patterns on these pages straight from the book (step 1). Alternatively, you can make them larger or smaller on a photocopier if you wish, and then follow steps 2–4.

Ask an adult to help you enlarge the patterns on a photocopier.

1 Place a piece of tracing paper over the pattern, then tape it down with small pieces of masking tape. Trace around the outlines using a soft pencil.

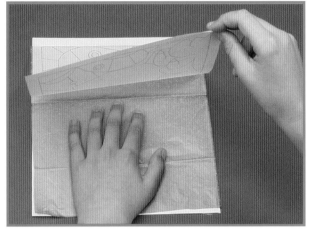

2 Place the tracing paper or photocopy on the surface of the project and tape it at the top. Slide the transfer paper underneath and tape it at the bottom.

3 Trace over the outlines with the pencil, pressing down firmly.

4 Remove the tracing paper, and the transfer paper, to reveal the design.

Pattern for the Fruity
Flower Pot featured
on pages 22–23.

Pattern for the
Bumble Bee
Spoon featured
on pages 10–11

Pattern for the Sun Wall Hanging
featured on pages 14–15.

Pattern for the Monster Egg featured on pages 24–25.

Pattern for the Padlocked Money Box featured on pages 18–19.

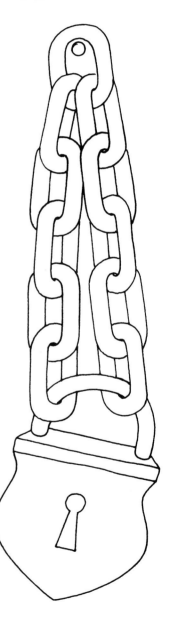

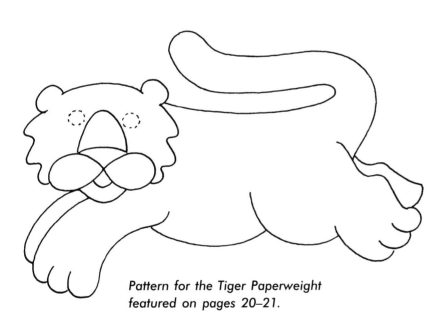

Pattern for the Tiger Paperweight featured on pages 20–21.

Pattern for the Picasso Mirror featured on pages 26–27.

Index